Timeline of Ancient Rome

8th century BC

Archaeological evidence suggests that the city of Rome was founded around this date as settlements and villages gathered near a ford on the river Tiber grew together.

3rd century BC

Rome fights the city-state of Carthage for control of the Mediterranean. By defeating Carthage and conquering its territories, Rome becomes an imperial power with control over Sicily, the Iberian Peninsula and Africa.

509 BC

The Roman Republic is established when the last king of Rome, Tarquin the Proud, is deposed and replaced with a system of elected magistrates and representative assemblies, where Roman citizens can vote on decisions.

1st century BC

Julius Caesar uses political cunning and military power to conquer Gaul, command respect in Rome and become ruler of the divided empire.

27 BC

Octavius, or Augustus, comes into power and the era of the Roman Empire begins. He ushers in a golden age of art, literature, wealth and peace.

476 AD

After several centuries of civil wars and barbarian invasions, Romulus Augustus, last emperor of the Roman Empire, is removed from power. This marks the end of Ancient Rome and the beginning of the Middle Ages.

44 BC

Caesar is assassinated and Rome is once again plunged into political turmoil.

Roman soldiers' barracks

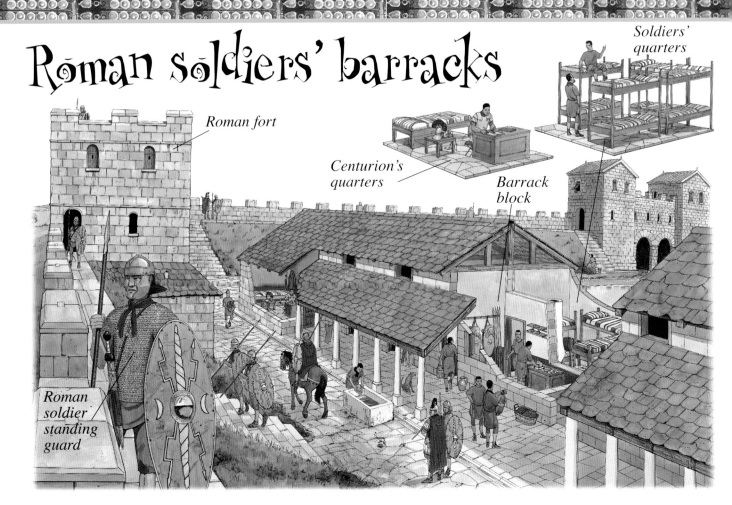

Soldiers' quarters

Roman fort

Centurion's quarters

Barrack block

Roman soldier standing guard

A fort for a cohort of around 500 soldiers has six barrack blocks, each containing the living-space for a century of 80 men. Barrack blocks are long and narrow, with the living quarters for the centurion in command at one end. The foundations are made of stone, and the upper parts have a framework of wood, filled in with rubble and plastered over. The roof is covered in tiles, stone slates or wooden shingles, depending on what materials are available locally.

The centurion has the luxury of several rooms to himself, including a separate bedroom and living room. The living quarters for the rest of the troops are much more cramped, with only two small rooms for every eight men. They use one room for sleeping, and the other is used for storing their equipment.

Author:
David Stewart has written many non-fiction books for children. He lives in Brighton with his wife and son.

Artist:
David Antram was born in Brighton, England, in 1958. He studied at Eastbourne College of Art and then worked in advertising for fifteen years before becoming a full-time artist. He has illustrated many children's non-fiction books.

Series Creator:
David Salariya was born in Dundee, Scotland. He has illustrated a wide range of books and has created and designed many new series for publishers both in the UK and overseas. In 1989, he established The Salariya Book Company. He lives in Brighton with his wife, illustrator Shirley Willis, and their son Jonathan.

Editor: **Sophie Izod**

Consultant: **Stephen Johnson**
Director of Operations, Heritage Lottery Fund, and author of several books on Roman archaeology.

Published in Great Britain in MMXVI by
Book House, an imprint of
The Salariya Book Company Ltd
25 Marlborough Place, Brighton BN1 1UB
www.salariya.com

ISBN: 978-1-910706-45-9

SCRIBO BOOK HOUSE SCRIBBLERS

3 5 7 9 8 6 4 2

A CIP catalogue record for this book is available from the British Library.
Printed and bound in China.
Reprinted in MMXVIII.

Visit
www.salariya.com
for our online catalogue and
free fun stuff.

PAPER FROM
SUSTAINABLE
FORESTS

You Wouldn't Want to Be a ™
Roman Soldier!

At least we're seeing the world!

Written by
David Stewart

Illustrated by
David Antram

Created and designed by
David Salariya

Barbarians You'd Rather Not Meet

BOOK HOUSE

Contents

Introduction — 9

Joining up — 10

Training to be a legionary — 12

Your first battle — 14

Return to Rome — 16

All at sea — 18

Left, right, left, right! — 20

Hadrian's Wall — 22

Life in the Fort — 24

Day-to-day life — 26

Battle the Barbarians! — 28

Illness and injury — 30

Promotion, retirement, death — 32

Glossary — 34

Index — 36

Introduction

The year is AD 105 and the Roman Emperor Trajan is fighting against the barbarians on the Danube. You are Marius Gaius who at the age of eighteen joined the army to become a Roman soldier. The Roman army invades and conquers foreign lands extending the frontiers of the Empire. These lands are called provinces and all must send tributes and taxes to Rome. By the second century AD people living on the edge of the Arabian deserts, in north Africa or in Britannia (Britain) can call themselves Roman citizens. As a Roman citizen who can speak Latin, you join the army as a legionary soldier. Joining the army will change your life forever bringing you hard work, danger and excitement. But not everyone can join the army like you – slaves are not free to join. Soldier's pay varies from one unit to another. At the time of Emperor Hadrian (AD 117-138) legionary soldiers are paid about 300 silver denarii each year.

Map of the Roman Empire

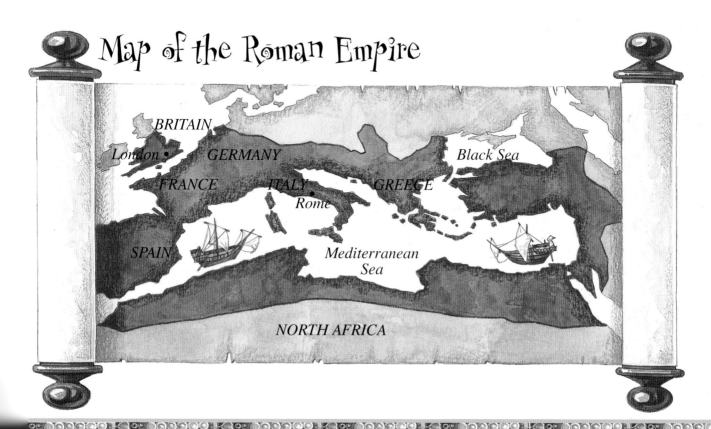

BRITAIN

London •   GERMANY

FRANCE   ITALY   GREECE   Black Sea

Rome •

SPAIN   Mediterranean
Sea

NORTH AFRICA

Joining up

A soldier's life is tough so why would you want to enlist? You might die in battle or from diseases caught on campaign. Even when you are not fighting you will spend long hours training or building roads and forts. Food is simple and discipline is harsh so why become a soldier? One reason is that you will be paid fairly well and regularly. Soldiers also get a share of booty and a generous pension when they retire. There is a good chance of promotion and its a great way to escape a dull, routine life.

YOU CANNOT JOIN the army if you are a slave or if you are less than 1.75 metres tall. Sons of old soldiers are especially welcome. Once in the army many men never see their homeland again.

As soon as I am tall enough, I am going to join the army!

You need to be 18 years old, too!

Swearing the oath

THE MILITARY OATH. When you arrive at the recruitment camp you swear an oath which binds you to the army for 25 years, or until you die.

BUY YOUR UNIFORM. Equipment used by legionaries is mass produced in the eastern lands of the Roman Empire. The cost of your uniform, weapons, bedding, rations, a share in the tent, and the unit's burial fund will all be taken from your pay.

Legionary infantry

Helmet

Handy hint

You carry your own
essential kit – a saw, a
hook, a rope, a pick-axe,
and much more. Make
sure you pack
carefully.

Armour made
of metal strips

Essential kit

Sword

Leather stomach
protector

Woollen tunic

Spear

Leather sandals

Cretan
archer

Balearic
slinger

Auxiliaries:

AUXILIARY SOLDIERS
were originally recruited from
non-Roman tribes. Their name
means 'helpers', and they assist
Roman legionary troops by
providing extra manpower and
specialised fighting techniques.
They fight using armour and
weapons from their native lands.

Training to be a legionary

A Roman legion is made up of...

8 men = 1 contubernium

10 contubernia = 1 century

2 centuries = 1 maniple

6 centuries = 1 cohort

The Roman Imperial army has about 150,000 soldiers, called legionaries, who join the army for life. They sign on for 25 years service. Your army life begins with training in Rome. You are taught how to march, how to build a camp and you must drill twice a day. Your main training is in the use of weapons and you are taught how to fight. You are in a group of eight men called a contubernium (a tent group). A century (80 men) is made up of ten such groups with a leader called a centurion.

Road building

ROMAN roads are built by ordinary soldiers. They form a vital network across the Roman Empire.

Our word 'military' comes from the Latin for soldier.

Horse riding!

Wrestling!

LEGIONARIES are taught to ride, wrestle and to swim. Training battles are always dangerous and bloody. It's hard work but you survive . . . just!

Swoooooooosh!

Handy hint
Remember your sword is still sharp along its edges. It's only the point that is covered!

THE TRAINING GROUND
A post is set up for you to practice. You use real swords and spears, but the tips are covered.

Running!

We're supposed to be stabbing and thrusting at it!

He thinks he's chopping firewood!

0 cohorts = 1 legion (too many to fit on this page!)

Your first battle

You and the other recruits are sent to the Danube – your first post abroad. Emperor Trajan has decided to enlarge the frontiers of the Empire. The frontiers in this area have not changed since the time of the Emperor Augustus, 94 years ago and Trajan thinks the time is right for another advance. He plans to declare war against the Dacians. This will act as a warning to those tribes outside the Roman Empire who think its lack of expansion is a sign of weakness. Drobeta is a wealthy Dacian city (in modern day Romania) on the Danube. If captured it will provide the Imperial Treasury with a large profit.

War machines:

Ballista

The wooden posts didn't fight back!

14

Onager

ONAGER (left) Rocks are loaded into a sling fixed to a wooden arm. Twisting a rope will winch the arm back before being released and firing the rocks.

Handy hint

Keep well clear when the onager is being fired – you could go with it!

BATTERING RAM (left) For knocking holes in the enemy walls. Soldiers inside are well protected by the strongly made sides and roof.

Battering ram

Testudo (tortoise)

SOLDIERS (below) make a 'tortoise' formation by overlapping their shields to form a strong defensive shell.

15

Return to Rome

You have survived your first real battle, and have been lucky to return from the Danube with Dacian prisoners and the treasures you captured. Every Roman loves a good show. One of the very best is when a triumphant army returns to Rome and puts on a triumph, or victory parade. The Roman Emperor rides in a gilded chariot and the procession winds through the streets and the Forum to the Capitol. This is where animals are sacrificed to the Roman gods Venus, Mars and Victory and here the chief prisoner (usually the enemy leader) may be executed.

Prisoners

PRISONERS (above) are sold in the slave market. Throughout the Roman empire there are millions of slaves who have no rights at all. Families are split up and sold separately. Strong, fit men are sold to be trained as gladiators (below).

Victory parade:

THE STREETS OF ROME are packed with crowds. The senators lead the parade, followed by row upon row of troops. Treasures captured in battle are carried shoulder high and soldiers lead white oxen to be sacrificed at the Temple of Jupiter. The crowds cheer as enemy leaders are displayed in chains.

Handy hint

To keep him humble a slave holds a laurel wreath above the Emperor's head and whispers in his ear "Remember that you are only a man."

"Io triomphe!"
(Behold the triumph!)

17

All at sea

Time passes, but there is no rest for the soldiers. You have fought in many campaigns, and as an experienced soldier you are sent to Britannia (Britain). The Roman Empire has a new Emperor now, Emperor Hadrian. It is Hadrian's policy not to expand the Empire but to strengthen its existing frontiers. He wants his army to be highly efficient and is introducing reforms to make auxiliary troops serve far away from their country of origin.

The Imperial Navy

THE ROMAN NAVY plays its part in wars. Ships are used to carry men and horses to fight in distant lands. Julius Caesar had 600 special landing craft and 28 warships built to help with his invasion of Britannia in 54 BC. But sea travel is difficult and has to be done during the summer.

Are we nearly there yet?

Left, right, left, right!

After a long sea journey you arrive in Britannia. You march north along roads built by other soldiers. Roads are built to suit the army, not the local people. They are usually as straight as possible, connecting important military centres. Soldiers march in strict order – cavalry at the front, then infantry, then the baggage train followed by the very best troops. It is necessary to make marching camps, temporary overnight camps to rest in. Northern tribes have resisted the Roman invaders and the previous legion which fought them has been wiped out. To stop the tribes attacking his troops and settlements, Hadrian has decided to build a long wall across the most easily defended part of Britannia.

We're on guard, so no tent for us tonight!

BASIC DIET is hard, dry bread with lard, washed down with vinegar or sour wine. When they're available you might also have lentils, beans, cabbage, mutton, lamb, beef, hare, goat, and deer. If you're lucky, you might even have some locally caught fish.

MARCHING makes the legionaries strong and fit. Distances of 25 or more kilometres must be covered at a quick pace in five hours. You would also carry twenty kilograms of equipment.

SANDALS (right) have heavy studs on the soles to prevent the leather wearing down quickly.

Handy hint

Try to get a space in the middle of the tent, it's the warmest and driest position.

Tents are made of leather, with straw on the floor.

Hadrian's Wall

Once built, Hadrian's Wall is 117 kilometres long. It stretches from Bowness-on-Solway on the west coast to Wallsend-on-Tyne in the east. The wall is six-and-a-half metres high, three metres thick and takes six years to complete! It is built by legionaries and marks the northern boundary of the vast Roman Empire. To the north of the wall lies a deep defensive ditch designed to keep the unconquered tribesmen out, and to the south is a vallum, which is a large ditch flanked by huge mounds of earth. It is manned by 10,000 auxiliary soldiers from across the empire, and you're soon put to work building forts large enough to house men, horses, weapons, and supplies.

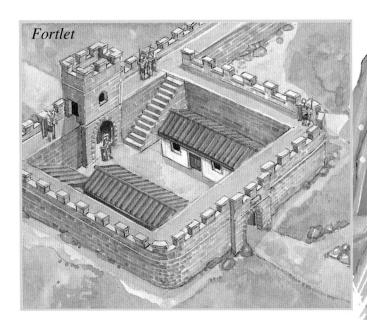

Fortlet

THERE ARE a total of 16 forts along the length of the wall. Fortlets (above) are built every 1.6 km with signal towers every 530 metres between them.

EMPEROR HADRIAN ordered the building of the great wall after his visit to Britain in AD 122. The work began in the east.

Hadrian's Wall

Handy hint

Ask a scribe to write home for underwear. Romans do not usually wear it, but a winter spent on the freezing wall soon changes old habits.

Life in the Fort

Luckily for you, once the Wall is complete you return to your well-appointed barracks in Chester, 160 km to the south. Soldiers are not always fighting so you have regular training sessions to keep fit. Life for legionaries and auxiliaries is much the same. Weapons need cleaning, animals need feeding, wood for fires needs cutting, and braziers need to be kept lit. The job of cleaning the latrines (lavatories), is usually given as punishment so try to avoid it!

Who's on latrine cleaning duties this week?

Keeping clean:

ROMAN LATRINES (below) Seats are placed over a channel, flushed with running water. Washable sponge sticks are shared because there is no such thing as toilet paper yet!

BATH HOUSES Bathing is an important part of Roman life all over the empire. Baths are a good place to meet friends, gossip, and relax.

Latrines

Baths

Day-to-day life

Local people hated the Wall and its forts when they were built. But they soon realised that there was money to be made from the newly arrived and relatively well-paid soldiers. Some local chiefs make an alliance with Rome to help fight their old tribal enemies. Villagers provide all kinds of services, from food and clothes to taverns to relax in. They also feel much safer being so close to such a large number of soldiers and are grateful that these troops – backed up by your legion's extra muscle when needed – can protect them from attack. No serving soldier in the Roman army – legionary or auxiliary – is allowed to marry because of the long periods of time they must spend away from wives and children. However, many lonely soldiers choose local women as wives and rent houses outside the fort to live in and raise families. The army refuses to recognise these 'unofficial' marriages until you complete your service, but everyone else does!

Getting friendly:

A LOCAL GIRL catches your eye and after romancing her, the two of you fall head-over-heels in love.

NOT EVERYONE IS HAPPY for you though. Your superiors disapprove and urge you to end the relationship.

MARRIED! Ignoring their advice, you wed the girl of your dreams. However, she will have to live outside the fort.

Handy hint

Try to sneak past the sentries and get away from the fort as often as possible to see your wife and family. Keep your eyes open!

Battle the Barbarians!

A messenger arrives at your fortress – you and your fellow legionaries are needed to help defeat an attack by a large group of Brittones! It's a four-day-march back to Hadrian's Wall and you arrive to find a heated battle underway. In the front line, you hurl your spear at the enemy – a strong soldier can throw his spear over 25 metres – and then move in for hand-to-hand fighting using swords. This is the most dangerous time for a Roman soldier and many are injured. Before you know it, you too are wounded!

Who'd have thought it would end like this?

THE ROMANS and the Brittones both lik collecting their enemies' heads as trophie

Know your enemies:

Raaaargh!

Handy hint

Avoid falling into enemy hands. Not all local ladies are kind and gentle.

THE TRIBES OF BRITTONES (Britons) make life on the frontier as difficult as possible for the Romans. They use ambushes and often attack in small groups before retreating so they don't get caught. Sometimes they even get inside a Roman fort and burn it down.

Illness and injury

Each fort has a team of medical staff trained to provide emergency treatment and hospital care. Army doctors are highly respected and are assisted by dressers who treat wounds during a battle and nurse the injured soldiers back to health. Common battle wounds include jagged sword cuts, broken bones, and dislocated joints. Doctors clean wounds and stitch them together, they also sometimes have to amputate damaged limbs. Salt, turpentine, and arsenic are used as antiseptics to stop wounds becoming infected. You're in good hands because Roman army doctors can give you excellent medical care.

SPEAR POINTS and arrowheads (below) sunk deep into the flesh are difficult to remove and treat.

DRESSERS give first aid on the battlefield.

WELL-PLANNED HOSPITALS are an essential part of every fort (right). As well as operating tables and beds for soldiers to recover on, they also prepare all the medicines and bandages here.

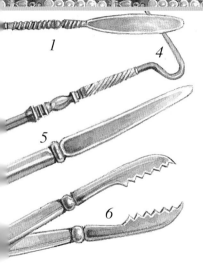

Medical instruments

1 Spatula (knife for spreading ointment)
2 Tweezers
3 Probe used for shallow wounds
4 Hook
5 Knife used for surgery
6 Forceps

Handy hint

Drink alcohol as a way to numb pain during surgery. Be careful though, alcohol thins your blood so you will bleed more.

Relax - this won't hurt...well, not much anyway.

GRIMACE AND BEAR IT. Bite down on a piece of wood as the doctor operates to stitch and clean the wound. It's agony, but there is no anaesthetic to numb the pain.

LUCKILY YOU make a full recovery, and your wife and son welcome you home. Any soldiers too weak to fight are retired.

Promotion, retirement, death

After a full recovery you return to army life, and soon your mind turns to promotion. As you come from an ordinary Roman family, you must work hard to prove you have what it takes to become a legionary centurion – one of the most important ranks in the army. This means showing skill and courage in battle as well as leadership. You'll never achieve the highest rank in the army though – that belongs to the Emperor!

AS WELL AS FIGHTING, centurions have daily meetings to report any problems and are responsible for ordering fresh supplies.

PASSWORDS. Roman forts were targets for enemy spies. To stop them from infiltrating the fort, change the *tessera* or password, daily (below).

AVCRIB

Two ways to become a centurion

THE EASY WAY: Be born into a wealthy family.

THE HARD WAY: Start at the bottom and work your way up.

Signifier (standard bearer)

Legatus (commander of a legion)

Tribune (staff officer)

Handy hint

It's been so long since you left home that there's no point in returning – nobody would remember you!

Rank and file

ON YOUR journey up the career ladder you have been both a tribune and a standard bearer, but sadly you never made Legatus – if you had, you could have been made governor of a Roman province when you retired.

What can you look forward to?

REMEMBERED When you die, your proud son erects a tombstone in your honour.

SHARE A DRINK and swap stories with other retired soldiers and friends.

GIFT OF LAND After 25 years of service and numerous scars, you retire honourably. The army gives you some land on which you can build a home and start a farm. But farming is hard work – there's no chance to relax for you!

Glossary

Alliance An agreement to co-operate between two or more groups of people.

Amputate When a limb is so badly damaged that all or part of it has to be cut off.

Anaesthetic A substance that reduces the feeling of severe pain.

Antiseptic Something that reduces the likelihood of infection by killing germs.

Arsenic A very poisonous substance used by Romans to treat infections. It is very dangerous.

Auxiliary Soldiers recruited from local areas either inside or outside the Roman Empire.

Ballista A large catapult used to hurl objects such as spears or rocks at enemies.

Barbarian The name given to another nation or civilisation the Romans considered more primitive.

Brazier A metal pan containing hot coals which were used to provide heat.

Britannia The Roman name for Britain.

Brittones The Roman name for the tribes in the area of Hadrian's Wall.

Century A unit of 80 men in the Roman army.

Dacians People from what is now modern-day Romania.

Danube A river that flows through a number of countries in Europe. It was one of the frontiers of the Roman Empire.

Denarii Roman units of currency.

Depose To overthrow or remove someone from power.

Forum An important meeting place in ancient Rome.

Laurel A bush whose leaves were used to make wreaths worn on the head to celebrate a victory. Only important Romans could wear them.

Legatus The commander of a legion. They are highly skilled and experienced officers.

Legionary A soldier in an army unit of about 4,800 soldiers.

Onager A device like a catapult that fired rocks at enemies.

Scribe Someone paid by the soldiers to write letters home. Many Roman soldiers could not read or write.

Tessera A Latin word meaning 'password.'

Triumph The name of the victory procession through Rome after an important battle had been won.

Turpentine A liquid made from the resin of trees which was used to treat infections. It is very dangerous and is not used as medicine today.

Index

A
antiseptics 30, 34
auxiliary soldiers 11, 20, 26, 34

B
ballista 14, 34
barbarians 9, 28, 34
barracks 25
bath houses 24
battering ram 15
Brittania 9, 18, 20, 34
Brittones (Britons) 28, 29, 34

C
centurion 12
century 12, 34
cohort 12, 13
contubernia 12

D
Dacians 14, 16, 34
Danube (River) 14, 16, 35
denarii 9, 35
diet 20
doctors 30

F
fort 26
fortlet 22
fortress 24

G
gladiators 16
gods 16

H
Hadrian, Emperor 9, 18, 20, 22
Hadrian's Wall 20, 22, 23

I
Imperial Navy 18

J
Julius Caesar 19

L
Latin 9, 12
latrines 24, 25
laurel wreath 17
Legatus 33, 35
legion 13
legionaries 10–13, 22, 26, 28, 35

M
maniple 12
marching camps 20–21
marriage 26
medical instruments 30–31
military oath 10

O
onager 15, 35

P
prisoners 16
promotion 32

R
roads 20

Roman Empire 9, 20, 22
Imperial Army 12
Legion 12
Romania 14

S
scribes 23, 35
senators 16
signal tower 22
signifier 12, 33
slaves 16–17
spears 11, 29, 31
swords 11, 28

T
tents 21
tessera 32, 35
testudo 15
training 10, 24
Trajan, Emperor 9, 14
Tribune 33
triumph 16–17, 35

U
underwear 23
uniform 10–11

V
vallum 22

W
wives, women 26–27

Romulus and Remus

Rome was associated with violence from its earliest days. According to legend, the great city was founded on 21st April 753 BC by the twin brothers Romulus and Remus. The brothers were said to be descendants of the Trojan prince Aeneas, and supposedly were raised by a she-wolf.

It is said that Romulus eventually killed Remus after the brothers quarrelled over who would rule. The city was then named after the victorious brother.

The story goes that, in need of people to populate the new city, the brothers invited the unwanted and the outcast to join them. Although the city was soon filled with workers, there were no women to produce future generations of inhabitants. Romulus embarked on missions to recruit women from neighbouring towns and villages, but he had trouble persuading them to live alongside the 'undesirables' already in Rome.

Famous Roman battles

The Second Punic War, 218-203 BC During this war between Rome and the city-state of Carthage, the Carthaginian general Hannibal led a force of soldiers and elephants over the Alps to conquer Italy. Hannibal's invasion of Italy lasted for 16 years and caused enormous disruption. Unfortunately for him, the Romans used tactics of guerrilla warfare to delay Hannibal's journey and diminish his army so that he was unable to carry out his plans.

The Battle of Pharsalus, 9th August 48 BC Julius Caesar and his allies met the republican forces of Pompey the Great at Pharsalus in central Greece. Outnumbering Caesar's soldiers, Pompey made the mistake of rushing into battle rather than waiting for the enemy to starve, and suffered a crushing defeat.

After the battle, Pompey escaped dressed as an ordinary citizen to avoid discovery.

The Battle of Philippi, 42 BC This was the final battle between Gaius Octavius (Augustus) and Mark Antony on the one hand, and Brutus and Cassius Longinus – the killers of Julius Caesar – on the other. War had been declared on the assassins as vengeance for their murder of the former emperor. Cassius' and Brutus' separate armies were defeated on two occasions at Philippi in Macedonia, and they both committed suicide.

The Battle of Actium, 2nd September 31 BC This naval battle between the ships of Gaius Octavius (Augustus) and the vessels of Mark Antony and Cleopatra was waged on the Ionian Sea near the city of Actium. When Antony's fleet of ships was destroyed, his army fled. Defeated, and believing Cleopatra to be dead, Antony stabbed himself. Octavius was able to use his victory to strengthen his control over Rome and become emperor.

The Battle of Adrianople, 9th August 378 AD An army led by the Eastern Roman Emperor Valens fought the Gothic rebels, an East Germanic barbarian people led by the chieftain Fritigern. The Roman forces suffered a catastrophic defeat, and the Emperor Valens was killed. As a result of their victory, the Goths were able to negotiate a settlement in their favour, including keeping their own independent territory within the Roman Empire.